20th Century Fashion

A Scrapbook-1900 to Today

1. *Title page:* If form followed fashion; the bustle (1904) the monobosom (1913), the hobble (1913), the concave hipless flapper (1920) Statuettes modelled by Constantino Nivola and designed by Bernard Rudofsky for his exhibition "Are Clothes Modern?" at the Museum of Modern Art, New York 1944

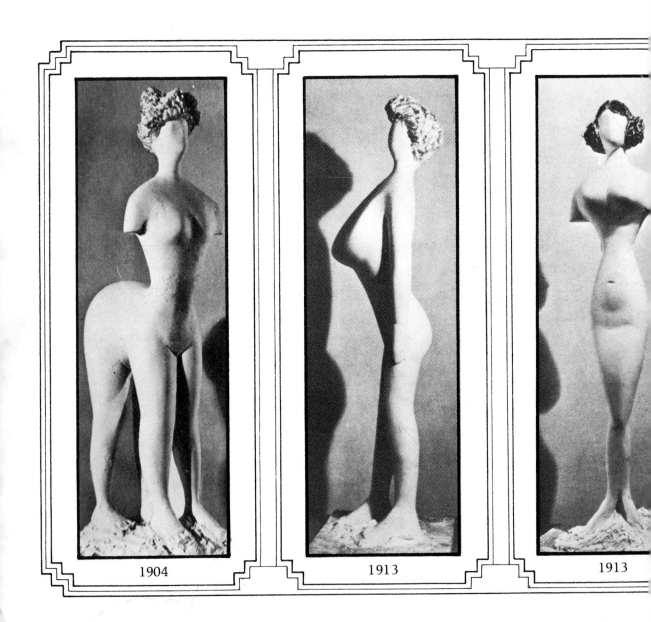

1904

1913

1913

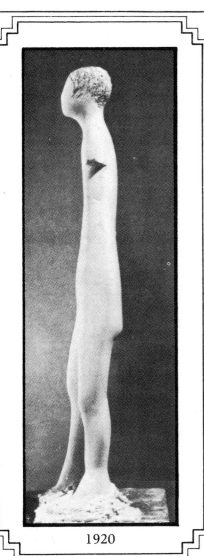

1920

Ernestine Carter

20th Century Fashion

A Scrapbook-1900 to Today

Eyre Methuen

First published 1975
by Eyre Methuen Ltd
11 New Fetter Lane, London EC4P 4EE
Copyright © 1975 Ernestine Carter
Printed in Great Britain by
Butler & Tanner Ltd
Frome & London

ISBN 0 413 33010 9

2. The cape, 1900/1

Contents

3. The cape,
by Jacques Fath, 1948

Picture Credits

Acknowledgements and thanks for permission to reproduce pictures are due to Mr Bernard Rudofsky for the frontispiece (from his book *The Unfashionable Body*)—to the Manchester Art Gallery for plate 2—to Popperfoto for plates 4, 33 and 132—to Snark International for plates 7 and 9—to the Victoria and Albert Museum for plates 10, 12, (*les Modes*), 17, 18 (*Gazette du Bon Ton*), 22, 27 (*les Modes*), 30 (*Femina*), 32 (*les Modes*), 38, 39, 40 (*Woman's Own Companion*), 56 (*les Modes*), 76, 77 (*Plaire*), and 119, 122 (*les Modes*)—to the Bibliothèque des Arts Décoratifs, Paris for plates 11, 16 and 20 (drawing by Sem)—to the Mander and Mitchenson collection for plates 13, 15, 31 and 51—to Bulloz for plates 14 and 25—to the Seeberger collection for plates 19, 21, 48, 53, 72, 74, 78, 79, 85, 86, 87, 88, 96, 98, 99, 106, 107 and 108—to the Tate Gallery for plate 24—to the Gernsheim collection for plate 26—to Moffett Co. Chicago for plate 29—to the Radio Times Hulton Picture Library for plates 28, 34, 46, 55, 73, 75 and 84—to Roger-Viollet for plate 35—to the Kobal collection for plates 36, 41, 61, 62, 64 and 80—to the Museum of Costume, Bath, for plates 42, 43, 45, 47, 113 (photo Eales), 120 (photo Hunt), 123, 125 (photo Lichfield), 134 (photo Hardin), 135 (photo Hardin) and 136—to the Duchess of Argyll for plates 44, 69 and 70—to French *Vogue* for plates 43, 45, 47—to *Vogue* for plates 8, 49 (drawing by Brunelleschi), 50, 65, 67, 68, 90, 91, 128 (photo Davies), 130 (photo Eales) and 133 (photo Hunt)—to Camera Press for plates 52 (photo Tom Blau), 54 (photo Hispard), 71 (photo Beaton), 112, 114, 115 (photo Hunt), 124 (photo Relang), 127 (photo Sam Levin), 131 (photo C. Black), 137 (photo G. Botti), 138 (photo Relang) and 139 (photo L. Gaunt)—to Associated Press for plate 57—to the British Film Institute for plates 59 and 60—to Selznick Properties for plate 63—to the Centre de Documentation du Costume, Paris, for plate 66—to *Harper's Bazaar* for plates 81, 82, 83, 89, 92, 93 (photo Kublin), 94 (photo L. Dahle-Wolfe), 95 (photo Avedon), 100 (photo R. Dormer), 103 (photo H. Clarke), and 110, 111 (photos Avedon)—to *The Sunday Times* for plate 97 (drawing by Crosthwait)—to Charles James for plate 101—to the John French collection for plates 102, 105, 117, 118 and 121—to Miss Conolly for plate 104—to J. Drysdale for plate 116—to John Stember for plate 123—to Alec Murray for plates 126 and 129—to Christian Benais for plate 136—to Saint Laurent for plate 140—to David Stetson for plates 141, 142, 144, 153 and 154—to P. Akehurst for plate 143—to Biba for plate 145—to Laura Ashley for plate 146—to Thea Porter for plate 147—to Gina Fratini for plate 148 (photo J. Allason)—to Zandra Rhodes for plate 149 (photo C. Arber)—to Clive Boursnell for plate 150—to Ben Coster for plate 151—to Richard Dormer for plate 152. Photographs taken by Eileen Tweedie and Miki Slingsby at the Victoria and Albert Museum and Jacqueline Hyde at the Arts Décoratifs, Paris. No copyright has been wittingly infringed in any picture reproduced in this book.

The picture on the front of the jacket is reproduced by kind permission of the *Daily Telegraph Magazine* (photo Terence Donovan) and that on the back by the Arts Décoratifs, Paris (photo J. Hyde).

Grateful thanks are due to Célestine Dars for the picture research throughout.

Introduction

1 January 1900: the dawn not just of a New Year but of a whole new century, the twentieth, the modern century. And what a century it turned out to be. It began with an unloosening of stays—literally and figuratively—and progressed to a more and more permissive society. It encompassed two World Wars; survived one Depression and teeters on the edge of another. Its early days were lit by the pyrotechnical burst of inventions of the last years of the Victorian age—the telephone, the electric light, the gramophone, the telegraph, the camera, the sewing machine, the cinematograph, the bicycle, the motor car, to be followed shortly by the overseas cable, colour photography and the flying machine.

As, from thrilling novelties, these became commonplaces of existence, they changed the shape of our lives—and the shape of fashion. The age of luxury gave way to the age of comfort, the age of leisure to the age of speed. The convenience era had begun.

1900 to 1908

With Queen Victoria's death in 1901, King Edward VII finally ascended the throne. The prudery and strict morals of the Victorian days were swept away on a flood tide of pleasure and prodigality. Once started, the relaxation of morals proved irreversible. Victorian mourning became Edwardian afternoon.

The Edwardian period was the last in which Court led fashion. Both the King and Queen were powerful trend-setters. Every hour of the day, every activity had its correct costume. Men as well as women changed their clothes half a dozen times a day, led in this strenuous schedule by Their Majesties.

There is, however, always a time-lag in fashion. Morals may have been loose but stays remained tight.

Modishness which had been considered the perogative of ladies of dubious virtue was encouraged. At last society could dress in the *dernier cri* from Paris, but the wearers were still encased from chin to toes, their necks in chokers or high boned collars, their bodies in cruel corsets, their waists laced to hand-span width. Above and below they pouched in front, protruded behind in what was called the S-bend. For evening, decolletages revealed a staggering expanse of monobosom. Hair was elaborately upswept, plumped out over pads of horsehair or even combings known unpleasantly as "rats". By day heads were topped with equally elaborate hats, skewered on with lethal hatpins, by evening with aigrettes.

Luxury and elaboration were the keynotes. The stuffy, heavy materials of the Victorians were abandoned for soft, pliant fabrics. "The Merry Widow" not only set everyone waltzing, its star, Lily Elsie, dressed by Lucile in chiffon and crêpe de chine, wonderfully worked and lavishly garnished with lace insertions, bead embroidery, ruffles, satin lover's knots, her finery balanced by the famous Merry Widow hat, became the toast of the town. The sober colours of the Victorians were replaced with the newly fashionable sweet pea shades.

4. Queen Alexandra, 1890, with the fringe and choker which she made fashionable

5. Edith Wharton furred and furbelowed in Paris

For day the tailor-made, which the English tailor, Redfern, had introduced to Paris, could be seen as the first step toward emancipation.

Across the Channel, Paris embroideries may have been more delicate and rich, Paris blouses more exquisitely tucked, Paris beading more bugled, but, beneath, smart Parisiennes, aristocrats and courtesans alike, were laced into the prevailing shape.

So were Americans, although on the pompadoured dollar Princesses portrayed by Charles Dana Gibson, the effect was fresher, crisper. The Gibson girl inspired by Irene Langhorne of Virginia (one of whose sisters became Lady Astor) was an outdoor rather than a hot-house flower.

The English Arts and Crafts Movement of the '90s had spread to the continent where as Art Nouveau it was introduced to an avid public at the French Exposition Universelle of 1900. To fit in with its sinuous lines, inspired by the waterlily and the lotus, ladies wore "picturesque" flowing garments. Art Nouveau,

6. Nancy, Lady Astor painted by her brother-in-law, Charles Dana Gibson, creator of the Gibson girl

however, except in jewellery, only remotely touched fashion.

Imprisoned as women were in a palisade of whalebone, to survive some breathing space was necessary. Between the fettered formality of afternoon dress and evening gown it became permissible to slip into something loose. These soft, sexy creations in filmy chiffon or fine silk, in England called tea gowns, in France *déshabillés* or *peignoirs*, were shown at that same World Fair in Paris (the first Exposition to include Fashion) where their daring attracted large crowds.

The tea gown, according to Janet Arnold, had already appeared in England as early as 1875. The next year in Paris Sarah Bernhardt was painted by Clairin wearing a long unshaped sheath, collared, cuffed and hemmed in ostrich fronds. (The divine Sarah was also a pioneer of trousers.) The tea gown, in the repellent fashionable slang of the day called a "teagie", reached its apogee after 1900. Seductive and intensely feminine, it was a harbinger of freedom to come.

SUCCÈS

PLASTIQUE

LIBELLULE

LUCIENNE

7. Corsets, 1908

12. Hopefully Art Nouveau, 1902

11427 C ROTARY PHOTO. E.C.   MISS LILY ELSIE.   FOULSHAM & BANFIELD

13. *above* Lily Elsie, the toast of the town in her "Merry Widow" hat, 1907

14. *right* Sarah Bernhardt painted by Clairin, wearing a precursor of the tea gown, 1876

15. Sarah Bernhardt, a pioneer of the pants suit, 1897

1909 to 1914

In 1909 the Ballet Russe burst upon Europe and immediately cast its spell of barbaric opulence over fashion and the fashionable world. Paul Poiret was the first designer to bring the seraglio into the Salon, the first to echo in his collections the violent primary colours of Bakst's sets and costumes. Other couturiers were pushed into the shade. Poiret, in Diana Vreeland's vivid phrase, became the Sultan of Fashion.

Poiret may not have been, as he asserted, the first to abolish the corset (a claim contested by both Vionnet and Lucile); he may not have invented the brassiere, although he certainly sponsored its adoption. But he did create the thin woman—a woman who could wear his slender dresses, dropping from a high waist below a soft bosom to a hobble skirt. The hobble was an anomaly. Perhaps he saw this garment, in which it was almost impossible to walk, as a symbol of luxury like the bound feet of the Chinese aristocrat. Using his vibrant palette, he created a galaxy of fantasies: tunics wired like lampshades, pantaloons, harem skirts. Richly embroidered, glittering in brocade, swathed

16. Typical Poiret turban and cloak, 1912. Drawing by Martin

in fur, they are preserved for us by the artists, Georges Lepape, Paul Iribe and Erté, all of whom worked in his studio.

Freeing women from their whaleboned trammels, Poiret set the course for contemporary fashion. Constriction only re-appeared twice in the years that followed—in the flattening brassieres of the '20s, and in the *guèpieres* or wasp waists of Dior's New Look of 1947. His influence was overpowering. Even Lucile followed him daintily into the harem, but other imitators were less successful.

Artists and those with artistic leanings were independent of fashion as were personalities like Lady Ottoline Morrell who dressed to suit herself.

In Chelsea, Augustus John set the Chelsea look of the day: full skirts gathered to a corselet, smock tops with full sleeves and floppy black felt hats. Still, eccentrics and artists were not in the main stream of fashion.

The bicycle had the dubious honour of giving birth to bloomers, named after the intrepid Mrs Amelia Bloomer who pioneered cycling for women. The motor car in its turn brought in its own paraphernalia: goggles, veils, wide-brimmed hats with soft cap-like crowns held on with long scarves, enveloping duster coats or capes (usually from Burberry), gauntleted leather or fur gloves.

The increasing appetite for sport began to modify clothing strictures although the athletes of the time, in their long volumin-ous skirts, seem incredibly bundled up to contemporary eyes. When swimming superseded bathing a more practical, though madly unbecoming, garment appeared, the one-piece swim suit named after Annette Kellerman, the first American aquatic star, who had introduced it in 1900. By 1910 it was accepted wear. Annette Kellermans were certainly more suitable for serious swimming than bloomered and skirted bathing suits, but, made in serge or wool (mistakenly thought to be warm), they weighed a ton when wet, and stayed wet for days. The greatest develop-ment in swimwear was not the bikini but the invention of light, fast-drying fabrics.

17. Typical Poiret tunic, 1912. Drawing by Georges Lepape

Another form of exercise also took the stage: the tango. Derived from South America, the tango dominated the dance floor in the years just before the War. Tangoing became addictive; dancing hours started at tea-time and carried on to dawn. One by-product was the gigolo, for expert partners were necessary to guide the tango-mad ladies through the intricate gyrations. Tango skirts were the wear—still ankle-length but slit up in front, to show tango slippers ribbon-laced from instep to above the ankle. The gigolos looked as South American as possible with long sideburns and greased black hair; the ladies took to turbans and pallor, rimmed their eyes in kohl, painted their lips dark red, waved cigarettes in long holders.

The sultry rhythms of the tango were followed by the syncopation of ragtime, a strictly American importation. By 1911 London and Paris were jigging in the Bunny Hug, the Turkey Trot, the one-step, the two-step and the foxtrot as demonstrated by the dance team of Irene and Vernon Castle. The gigolos transformed themselves from Latin Lovers into lounge lizards, imitating Vernon Castle's blonde English elegance. The women copied Irene Castle's slim chic and short hair which she had been the first to bob in 1913.

The Castles had numerous followers, but only Leonora Hughes of Maurice and Hughes in the late '20s equally influenced fashion, and that in a roundabout way. Where Mrs Castle had worn draped tunic dresses inspired by Poiret, Leonora Hughes's were by Patou: full-skirted chiffon dresses trimmed with ostrich feathers, a style later resuscitated for Ginger Rogers in the '30s.

But it was not only in nightclubs and restaurants that the world danced. In flats and houses carpets were rolled back and Victrolas blared, only pausing when they had to be wound up. Dancing became an integral part of life.

18. Tango skirt by Bakst executed by Paquin, 1912

19. 20. 21. The reality (1911), the caricature (1914), the dream (mannequins at Deauville, 1913)

565

ROBE DU SOIR, PAR LUCILE

22. Lucile follows the Ballet Russe, 1914

23. Lady Ottoline Morrell by Augustus John, c. 1926

24. The Chelsea Look: Dorelia by Augustus John, c. 1908

25. *overleaf* Bicyclists in the Bois de Boulogne, by Béraud, 1900

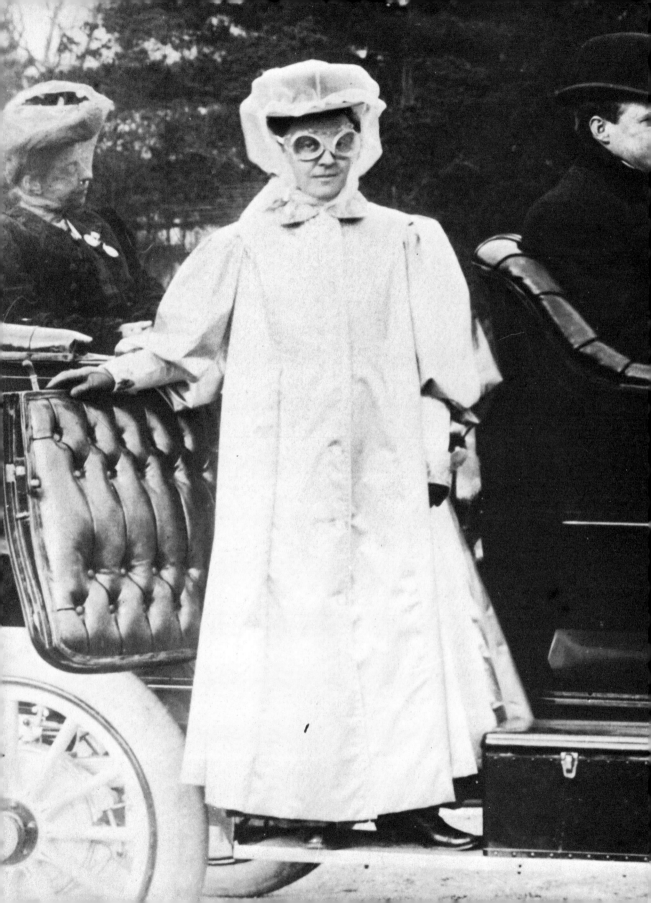

6. *left* Geared for motoring, *c.* 1905

7. *above* Accoutred for flying, 1910

28. Suited for swimming, Annette Kellerman, pioneer of the one-piece suit named after her

29. The Castles, 1915

30. The tango slipper

THE LATEST FASHION : "Pour Passer le Temps."

WHAT NEXT? TANGO TEAS AT THE QUEEN'S THEATRE, LONDON

DRAWN BY F. MATANIA

The novelty of the hour is the tango tea. It may be seen at the Queen's Theatre, London, with the stalls removed and replaced by tables and chairs for afternoon tea. The band is on the stage, where M. Clayton and Mlle. Marquis give us tango dances, and this is supplemented by a dress parade of all the latest fashions

31. A tango tea in London, drawn by F. Matania, 1913

32. Lady Sarah Wilson, author of *South African Memories* in her costume
inspired by the siege of Mafeking, 1909

The Civilian at War
1914 to 1918

The Declaration of War in 1914 extinguished what Michael Holroyd has called "the last brilliant afterglow of Edwardian England". The sewing machine had foretold the era of mass production which came really into being during the War. The Edwardian era had begun the dominance of the Couture; the sewing machine was slowly to erode it. Fashion was no longer to be the prerogative of the few; it was to belong to the many.

Women had already been moving toward greater freedom before the first War, in fact before the turn of the century. The suffragettes had begun their heroic fight to obtain votes for women against the apathy of their own, and the antipathy of the other, sex. Even earlier there had emerged "The New Woman", anything but a Woman's Libber: a serious, Fabian, Shavian sort of female, the bicycle her symbol, the tailored suit her badge. The War contributed to her emancipation as she took over more and more jobs previously allocated to men. Those not in uniform also found their feet. The narrow skirt quietly expired, the Poiret tunic growing longer while the tight under-skirt disappeared.

33. Knickerbockers and puttees for the Land Girl, c. 1915

34. Civilian dress influenced by uniforms, 19

The Twenties

After the Armistice there was a frenetic desire to forget the War. Dancing was continuous, drugging became fashionable, as did Negroes after the success of the review, ''The Blackbirds''. Sophistication was the word. From America, where Prohibition had brought in bootleg hooch, came cocktails—and hangovers. In both countries girls reached for a cigarette. The Bright Young Things took over the scene.

Dixieland jazz, born in 1916, followed by the Blues, accelerated the dancing passion, and it was Jazz that finally shaped what we think of as the fashion of the Twenties. Short skirts spelled the doom of the statuesque beauty who was ousted by the skinny little flapper. They also reduced underwear to bare essentials: the ''teddy'', a brief composite of petticoat and pantie. Stockings were rolled, for there was nothing to fasten them to.

But before the Charleston lifted skirts, hemlines betrayed the general post-war confusion, going up and down like a fever-graph, zigzagging in handkerchief points, dropping to the floor at the back, curving up in front, ludicrously in crinolines, called ''robes de style'', or camouflaged by transparent overskirts.

The waist meanwhile had dropped to the hips. With the bosom flattened out of existence and the widest part of even the slimmest female figure mercilessly accentuated, these clothes were anathema to those who wore them, irresistible to today's young.

Hair was shingled at the back, brought forward over the cheeks in what were vulgarly called ''spit curls'', more felicitously ''kiss curls'' or ''croche-coeurs''. The finger wave ousted the marcel, and a strange and awesome tangle of wires and bobbles produced frizzy permanent waves. Eyebrows were plucked into lines of perpetual astonishment. Cupid's bow mouths were outlined in bright red. Nails were red too after Peggy Sage brought out the first coloured nail-varnish. Legs were cased in pale silk stockings. Elinor Glyn invented ''It'' and Clara Bow was its film incarnation.

The simple shifts of the Jazz Age were hung with a mass of jewellery, real or fake: long and many strings of pearls, dangling ear-rings, diamond clips, lapel pins, and for the Blondes that Gentlemen Preferred diamond bracelets, as many as possible, dubbed, in deference to their presumed method of acquisition, "service stripes". For those who couldn't afford real rocks, Chanel had made fakes respectable.

Hats were deep *clôches*, coats were unfastened and, as they had to be hugged round, handbags shrank into inconvenient envelopes called *pochettes* or "sous le bras". *Bateau* necks were on the horizon, completing a welter of French words which, like "brassière" and "demi tasse", were unlikely to have been heard in France.

Chanel was *the* designer of the Twenties but as her influence lasted till her death in 1971 we have given her a special place. Madeleine Vionnet was the greatest dressmaker. Fagotting was her signature; her massive contribution, the bias cut, a cut so subtle that it was thought uncopiable. But it was copied and in the '30s its clinging line, which clung to the body "like the paper to the wall" as the phrase went, was not only the uniform for cinema sex queens like Jean Harlow, but was so adopted by the Couture both in England and France that Bianchini Ferier developed a double-width satin to avoid the hitherto inevitable seam.

Cubism set its stamp on fashion as well as on canvas: on fabrics, knitwear, and accessories like powder compacts and cigarette cases. The talented crew of La Gazette de Bon Ton continued to dominate fashion illustration, but the camera was beginning to assert its own capacity. Arnold Genthe's photographs of the then unknown Greta Garbo are credited with convincing the Metro-Goldwyn-Mayer moguls that the Swedish girl was worth keeping.

Others who proved that the lens could be more powerful than the brush were Edward Steichen, Hoyningen-Huene and Man Ray.

35. *above* Josephine Baker in her first film, "Les Femmes des Folies Bergère", 1929

36. The Charleston dress: Joan Crawford in "Our Dancing Daughters", 1928

37. Vionnet's short fringed "shimmy" dress, 1925/6

38. Upcurved "robes de style", 1927

39. Godets and handkerchief points, 1927

40. Up in front and down at the sides, 1928

41. *opposite* Clara Bow: the ''It'' girl, 1927

42. Head-hugging hats and wrapround coats, 1928

43. Clips, bracelets and *rivière*, photographed by Hoyningen-Huene, 1928

44. *opposite* Margaret Wigan, later Duchess of Argyll, in taffeta after
Chanel, 1928

45. Vionnet's bias cut, 1928, photographed by Steichen

46. Cubism-inspired knitwear, 1928

47. Chanel's transparent overdress, 1920

48. Castillo's lace cage, 1965

49. The burnous and caftan of 1920 presage the rage for the exotic of over forty years later. Drawing by Brunelleschi

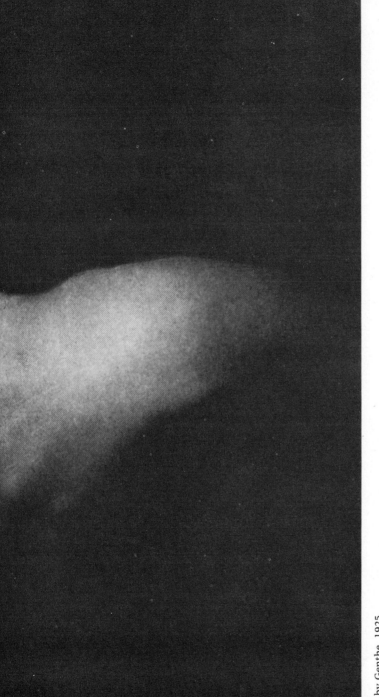

50. Garbo by Genthe, 1925

TH_ BATHING GROUND SEA VIEW, I .

SPORT

51. Bathing as it was, 1905
52. Bathing as it is

53. Skiing as it was, 1926
54. Skiing as it is

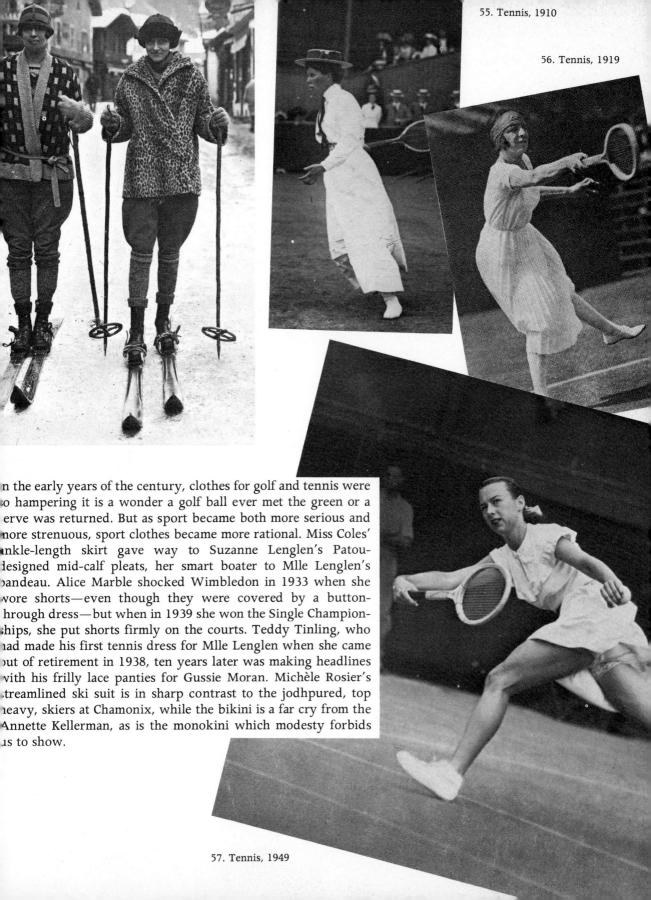

55. Tennis, 1910

56. Tennis, 1919

In the early years of the century, clothes for golf and tennis were so hampering it is a wonder a golf ball ever met the green or a serve was returned. But as sport became both more serious and more strenuous, sport clothes became more rational. Miss Coles' ankle-length skirt gave way to Suzanne Lenglen's Patou-designed mid-calf pleats, her smart boater to Mlle Lenglen's bandeau. Alice Marble shocked Wimbledon in 1933 when she wore shorts—even though they were covered by a button-through dress—but when in 1939 she won the Single Championships, she put shorts firmly on the courts. Teddy Tinling, who had made his first tennis dress for Mlle Lenglen when she came out of retirement in 1938, ten years later was making headlines with his frilly lace panties for Gussie Moran. Michèle Rosier's streamlined ski suit is in sharp contrast to the jodhpured, top heavy, skiers at Chamonix, while the bikini is a far cry from the Annette Kellerman, as is the monokini which modesty forbids us to show.

57. Tennis, 1949

58. Out and In: French Vogue greets the '30s

THE THIRTIES

The Stock Market crash of October 1929 and the succeeding Depression simply intensified the dancing. The Lindy Hop, the Big Apple and the Shag superseded the Charleston; to the tango was added the rumba, the samba and the conga. In the years between a depression and a War, there bloomed a golden age of music. The Merry Widow had entranced the Edwardians, the Ballet Russe the pre-War world. In the Thirties it was the songs of Jerome Kern, George Gershwin, Cole Porter and Noël Coward.

Films began to take a lead in influencing fashion. In Hollywood Adrian dressed the Metro-Goldwyn-Meyer stars, to each of whom he gave a style: Garbo with her page-boy hair-do, slouch hats and trench coats, Joan Crawford with her Letty Lynton sleeves, huge and puffed to show off her small waist, Jean Harlow with her slinky, bias-cut, halter-necked satin evening dresses. Garbo and Dietrich popularised slacks, more mannishly cut than the floppy pyjama suits of the Twenties. Theirs were the faces of the '30s.

The waist had returned to its normal place, skirts were a droopy mid-calf. The excitement was the backless dress, the inevitable was the fox fur, complete with head and tail.

After Elsa Maxwell had been hired to revive the Lido, resort life warranted a fashion of its own: beach dresses, beach pyjamas, close-fitting skirtless bathing suits, bare midriffs. In Capri Emilio Pucci, who had started his career after the War, was inventing a new way to look by the sea.

Wit was in the air. Surrealism was the new artistic sensation, Schiaparelli the new designer. Chanel with her monkey face had brought in the *belle laide*; Schiap a short, swarthy Italian, dispensed with the *belle*. Hard-edge chic was her forte, fantasy her speciality. Dali and Cocteau designed her prints, as did Christian Bérard, Drian and Vertès. She brought buttons to a new importance, making them into tremendous jokes—fishes, circus horses, stars. . . . "Amusing" was the height of praise, and Schiap was the amusing designer.

She came to London, where she opened her own house here in 1934, and saw the Guardsmen in their greatcoats. From them she took her padded, military shoulders, and wide lapels which she covered in barbaric gold embroidery. For evening she extended shoulders even farther with embroidered epaulets or sprays of aigrettes.

She invented "the little black dress", the long dinner suit, the evening sweater, was the first to use zips. Chanel had her Chanel N° 5, Schiap had her Shocking, a name she also gave to

THE FACES OF
THE THIRTIES

her favourite blue-pink.

Two other names reached fame in the Paris of the Thirties: each a foreigner. One was American Mainbocher, ex-Paris Vogue editor, ex-ready-to-wear designer, the other English Captain Molyneux, a graduate of Lucile. Their styles could not have been more different from Schiaparelli's. Each dealt in elegant understatement; each achieved world fame through Royal weddings—Molyneux designed Princess Marina's wedding dress when she married the Duke of Kent in 1934, and Mainbocher designed Mrs Simpson's when she married the Duke of Windsor three years later.

In England couture was being pioneered. By the Thirties the names of Norman Hartnell, Victor Stiebel, Digby Morton, Lachasse were known not just to England but to America as well. In America two women were establishing themselves as designers: the eccentric, individual, incredible Valentina and the brisk, original Elizabeth Hawes.

Then came the second War.

59. Garbo: the face of our times, 1929
60. Dietrich: the eternal, 1935
61. *overleaf left* Joan Crawford, 1932
62. *overleaf right* Jean Harlow, 1933

63. Joan Crawford in the famous Letty Lynton dress, 1932

64. Adrian dresses ''The Women'' (Joan Crawford, Norma Shearer, Rosalind Russell), 1939

65. *opposite* Schiaparelli's bare-back shocker, photographed by Steichen, 1932

66. Schiaparelli evenings, drawn by Christian Bérard, 1938

67. Schiaparelli dinner suit, drawn by Eric, 1937

68. The artists and photographer of the '30s: Bérard and
Eric photographed by Cecil Beaton

69. Margaret, Duchess of Argyll, in white crêpe by Victor Stiebel, 1930
70. Margaret, Duchess of Argyll, in her Presentation dress, by Norman Hartnell, 1930

71. The Duchess of Windsor, dressed for her wedding by Mainbocher, 1937

72. The look that lasted until Christian Dior: by Piguet, 1939

The Civilian at War
1939 to 1945

People said that nothing was the same after World War I. The same was true of World War II. In the two Wars life was fragmented, the pieces shaken around as if in a giant kaleidoscope. When the pieces settled, the patterns were inevitably different. Wars do not influence fashion; they change the social climate and fashion reflects that change.

Chanel and Schiaparelli closed their Houses. Molyneux returned to England, Mainbocher to America. Lucien Lelong, President of the Chambre Syndicale de la Couture Parisienne, succeeded in persuading the Germans not to transport the remaining Couture bodily to Berlin, although the clients were Fraus. The Parisiennes invented a fashion of defiance: towering turbans, short skirts (for bicycling), thick wooden soles and heels.

The British designers dispersed into the Forces. Clothes rationing froze fashion in the Schiaparelli silhouette of 1939. Even the Government-sponsored Utility (known as "Futility") clothing echoed this line.

America, isolated from its fount of inspiration, discovered its own designers, notably Hattie Carnegie and Claire McCardell, and Seventh Avenue came of age.

The Blitz put Englishwomen into trousers, their hair into kerchiefs. In 1942, in revolt, hair bounded high in front, dropped behind to the shoulders. Hair styles changed, but the kerchief became permanent headgear, even gaining Royal approval.

73. Utility clothes in England, 1943

74. Occupation fashion in Paris, 1942

75. Women on the land, 1943

The Forties

Just as the Thirties were truncated by the War, the Forties, in the sense of civilian life, did not start until 1945, and did not actually begin fashion-wise until 1947 with the debut of Christian Dior. This modest Norman re-established the dominance of Paris, and he himself dominated the scene until his untimely death in 1957. He was one of the few true geniuses of fashion.

Another, Spanish Cristobal Balenciaga, who had opened his Paris House in 1937, was shaping into the giant figure he became.

But it was Dior's New Look that captivated the world and made his name known overnight even to taxi drivers, school girls, and, most important, to the men who paid the bills. The flattery of his long, full, swinging skirts, tiny waspwaists, soft shoulders, the allure of his strapless evening dresses, restored femininity to a world sick of uniforms and uniformity.

Beneath the softness, however, was a carapace of construction, and Balenciaga's influence made its first popular impact when he released the body, first with gently shaped jackets, then with the totally unshaped Sack of 1957.

Other survivors from pre-War days were Lelong, Patou, Paquin, Grès, Schiaparelli, Lanvin and Nina Ricci. New names were the Greek Jean Dessès, Marcel Rochas, Jacques Fath and Pierre Balmain. Released from the anguish and hardship of War, and with subsidies from the Government, the French Couture seemed to swim in their new freedom like dazzling tropical

76. 77. The wartime silhouette persists:
right, Balmain, drawn by Pierre Simon, 1946;
below, Balenciaga, drawn by Drian, 1945

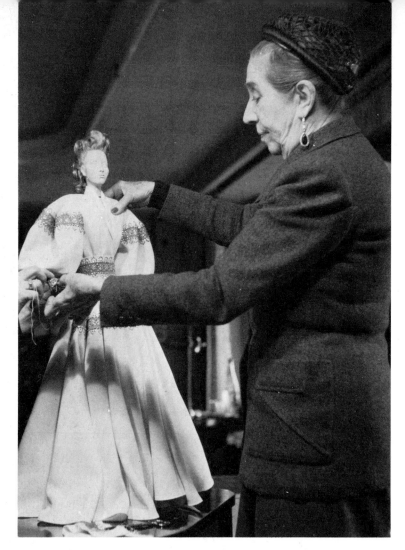

78. Madame Lanvin with her doll at the Théâtre de la Mode, 1945

fish. Elegance had not yet become a dirty word: clothes were beautiful, dramatic and sumptuous.

In England, The Incorporated Society of London Fashion Designers (originally founded in 1942) reassembled itself: Edward Molyneux, Norman Hartnell, Hardy Amies, Charlotte Mortimer (Worth), Digby Morton, Bianca Mosca, Peter Russell, Victor Stiebel and the newly elected Charles Creed.

Immediately after the War, the French Couture, to show the world that they were still in business, assembled a Théâtre de la Mode, a collection of dolls dressed by the couturiers. American manufacturers and buyers descended upon Paris like hungry birds pecking for the crumbs of inspiration that had been denied them so long. As the Forties eased into the Fifties, they were joined by the top British manufacturers who, before the War, had begun to reach for quality: Deréta, Dorville, Frederick Starke.

79. Square shoulders and the Hayworth hairdo,
sort of, Lanvin, 1946

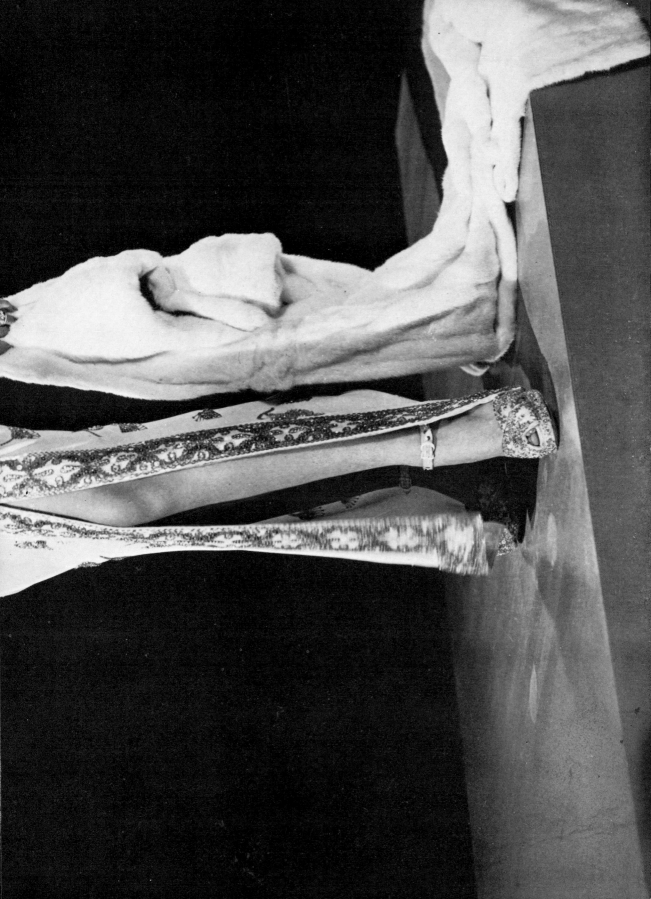

81. Christian Dior's New Look in dresses,
1947

84. New Look in coats, by Hardy Amies, 1949

. First New Look off the peg,
 Deréta, London, 1947

. Christian Dior's New Look in
ats, drawn by Demachy, 1947

87. 88. Opposing the New Look, the close-fitting dr
left by Piguet, 1948/49.
right by Jacques Fath, 1949/50

CHANEL

Gabrielle Chanel stands alone. Who else in fashion history has spanned more than half a century of activity (allowing for her time off from 1940 until she returned in 1954)? Who else has twice in a designing life put women into a uniform of her (or his) devising?

From World War I when she introduced sailors' pea jackets, and sweaters worn with her soon-to-be-famous sunray pleated skirts (she took over their pants, too, for yachting) to the "typical Chanel suit" that made her the most copied designer of the early '60s, her understanding of how women wanted to look at a given time was unerring.

Her clothes were the archetype of what came to be known as "understatement", the epitome of throwaway elegance. In the Twenties and Thirties she put her rich customers into jersey, hitherto a "poor" fabric. (She christened this specially woven jersey "kasha" after her favourite porridge colour.) She put them into casual cardigan jackets, into white silk or lawn shirts and shot their cuffs below her turned-back jacket sleeves—a trick she is said to have taken from Jean Cocteau. She put their feet into black sling-back pumps, toed in beige. She revived corduroy. She invented costume jewellery, started the vogue for suntan, and christened her scent with a name that became a by-word—Chanel N° 5. But her influence extended beyond clothes: she changed the whole stance of women from a pouter pigeon profile to an easy hips-forward, low-shouldered, hands-in-pockets slouch.

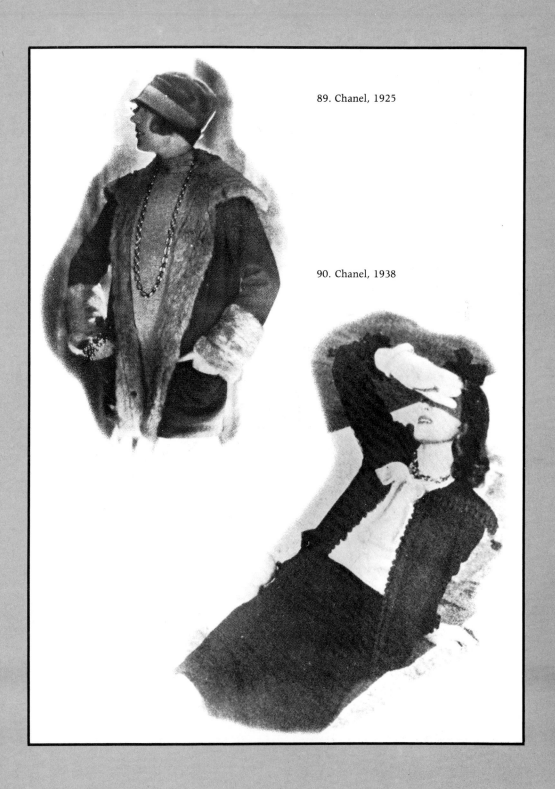

89. Chanel, 1925

90. Chanel, 1938

91. Chanel, 1954

92. Chanel, 1959

THE
FIFTIES

The Fifties got off to a slow start. Up to 1957 there was little change in the fashion scene. Dior continued his triumphant progress, producing new Lines to make headlines. 1956 was memorable for his one failure: his "demi-longeur", a length reminiscent of the Thirties. Undeterred, the next season he showed the short front and dipping back of the Twenties, an experiment which was to be repeated by Balenciaga the next year with greater success.

New names were Hubert de Givenchy, ex-Schiaparelli, and Pierre Cardin who opened their own Houses in 1955, and later Guy Laroche. By 1957 many of the great names, Chanel, Molyneux, Piguet, Lelong, Schiaparelli, Rochas, Fath, had become just labels on scent bottles. In 1958 the newest name of all swam into the fashion eye when the House of Dior presented Dior's successor: the youthful Yves Saint Laurent, who spun to immediate fame with his Trapeze Line.

Paris still held the unquestioned leadership, although the fashion map had been extended to Florence in 1950. Rome was soon to follow. Spain and Ireland, as well, were added to the fashion itinerary. Pucci was the star of Florence, Simonetta, Fabiani and Galitzine the leading lights of Rome with Capucci as the new boy wonder. Spain was Pertegaz and Ireland Sybil Connolly.

93. Dior's H Line, 1954

Lelong in the '20s had been the first couturier to launch into the ready-to-wear; Hardy Amies, the first in England—in 1951. His was also the first boutique in London.

The Fifties saw the greatest revolution in hair-styling since Antoine invented the pin curl. The first innovation was the roller, lifting the hair to provide a soft frame for the face, the lift sustained by strenuous back-combing. The second was hair spray which laquered the lift in place.

The third made its appearance in 1958 when Givenchy put his mannequins in wigs by Carita. Hats were doomed.

At the other end fashion was less happy. Peep-toes and platform soles had given way to paper-thin soles and tapering heels. The Italians developed a technique of strengthening their needlepoint heels with long steel nails. These stiletto heels were perhaps the most destructive fashion in history: pockmarking

94. Dior's A Line, 1955

parquet floors, wearing holes in priceless rugs, perforating aircraft, a gift to chiropodists.

On the credit side, nylon had changed the stocking picture. Warm skin tones added a cosmetic touch to legs, although in England fashion magazines continued to plug "seasonal" colours: beige, grey and flesh.

Behind this façade of fashion-as-usual, a revolution was brewing. The Beat Generation was beginning to assert itself. And like all revolutionary movements, right or left, it created its uniform: black stockings, short, bottom-hugging skirts, duffle coats, pale lips, long, uncombed hair. The Chelsea Look had arrived. A time-bomb started ticking when in 1955 Mary Quant opened her first Bazaar Shop in the King's Road to cater to the new independents. When it exploded it changed the fashion picture of the world.

95. *opposite* Balenciaga's belted jacket, 1950

96. Balenciaga's gentled jacket, 1957

97. The Sack by Givenchy, drawn by Crosthwait, 1957

98. Dior's second ''demi-longeur'', 1958

99. Givenchy's soft jacket, 1959

100. Spain's Pertegaz, 1953

101. Irish export to the U.S.A.: Charles James, 1957

102. Italy's Pucci

103. England's Stiebel, 1950

104. Ireland's Sybil Connolly finely
pleats Irish linen

105. America's Bonnie Cashin, the first with the layered look, photographed by John French, 1960

106. Castillo's Japanese-
inspired collection for
Lanvin, 1957

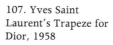

107. Yves Saint
Laurent's Trapeze for
Dior, 1958

108. Cardin's
blouse-backed jacket,

109. Balenciaga's lifted skirt, 1958

110. Givenchy's cuffed skirt, 1959

1. Balmain's ''Jolie Madame''
her joliest

The voice of the young had been becoming increasingly strident. In the Forties bobby soxers were shrilling at Frank Sinatra. In the Fifties they were squealing at Elvis Presley. In the Sixties Groupies found their idols in the Beatles. In the Seventies teeny boppers were mobbing the Osmonds.

A darker side of the youth explosion were the Mods and Rockers, the skin heads, the ton-up boys, the Hells Angels.

In 1960 their sound waves had percolated through the silken curtains of the House of Dior to the ears of Yves Saint Laurent, who presented a collection that blasted him out of his job, and incidentally presaged the decline of the Haute Couture. He was succeeded by Marc Bohan.

Perhaps sobered by this experience, Saint Laurent, when he opened his own House in 1962, reverted to conformity, and although he produced many pilot ideas, did not become a major influence until 1966 when he went into ready-to-wear with his Rive Gauche shop, the first of many.

The most original talent of the early Sixties was André Courrèges, a splinter off the Balenciaga block. Like Chanel, he created a uniform into which women fell with joy. The midi and the mood of softness combined to finish the domination of Courrèges's hard-edge idiom.

In 1964 Courrèges first took skirts to new heights. Mary Quant lifted them higher and the mini was born. The mini, dubbed by the *Evening Standard* "the gymslip of the permissive society", became the outward and visible sign of the generation gap which was yawning in morals and manners as well as clothes. The mini in its turn gave birth to tights (necessary to bridge another kind of gap). Underwear shrank to exiguous bras and briefs. Opposed to the sweater girls of the '50s, the new ideal was the androgynous Twiggy.

While skirts were rising, with splendid contrariness other legs were being hidden by trousers. Irène Galitzine in the late '50s had, with her lavishly embroidered palazzo pyjamas, made pants acceptable as evening wear. In New York Norman Norell in 1963 and in Paris Courrèges in 1964 were piloting trouser

112. *opposite* Fans at a Beatles concert, 1965

suits, to be followed in 1967 by Saint Laurent. Culottes had come first (in 1960). But it was the confusion of skirt lengths—mini, midi or maxi—that put women permanently into trousers.

The early Sixties were the years of extremities: hairdressers led by Alexandre and Carita in Paris, using wigs, hair pieces, falls, added literally a new dimension to fashion. Black became beautiful and Afro hair-cuts were adopted by whites as well. Unisex applied to hair (long for both sexes) as well as clothes. At the other end interest focused on legs and feet: on mad stockings and tights, on boots.

The Sixties did not begin to swing until 1965. Then they swung in all directions. Confused and worried, high fashion set out on a frantic search for inspiration. The designers looked around, they looked back; only Cardin seemed to look forward.

Every new film was culled for ideas from "Jules et Jim", "Bonnie and Clyde", to "Dr Zhivago". Westerns brought jeans. Art was not neglected and Mondrian gave Saint Laurent a brief success. Every national costume from gypsies to Eskimos was ransacked for ideas. Of ethnic dress, the caftan seems the most permanent. The astronauts provoked Courrèges and Cardin into moon-strike aberrations. The permissive society was apotheosised in the trend toward nudity. The pot era produced the Flower People, the Hippies and a new uniform of long-trailing printed dresses, bodiced in contrasting patterns. Sun specs became all-year wear.

Science has given fashion the means of total recall. Television and the vogue for old films plunged fashion into a seemingly endless bout of nostalgia. The Twenties, the Thirties, the Forties, the Fifties and even the Sixties have been resuscitated.

In England Mary Quant had become a national figure and an international star. Jean Muir was emerging as an important contemporary classicist. John Bates, Gina Fratini, Ossie Clark were establishing their handwritings. At the end of the Sixties Bill Gibb and Zandra Rhodes made dazzling debuts with daring forays into fantasy.

In Paris the couture was battling the rising tide of the ready-to-

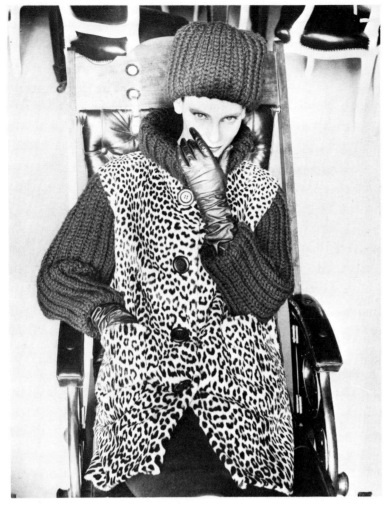

113. Yves Saint Laurent, innovator at Dior, 1960

wear. In Italy Valentino had reached top billing, but Missoni and Albini—both ready-to-wear—were nibbling at his heels.

Boutiques and discotheques sprouted everywhere, dark, and loud with canned music. Carnaby Street, the King's Road, and Biba became tourist attractions.

116. Twiggy and Twiggy mannequins, 1966

114. Courrèges's shorter skirt, 1964

115. Mary Quant's mini – and daisy tights, 1966

Adel Rootstein

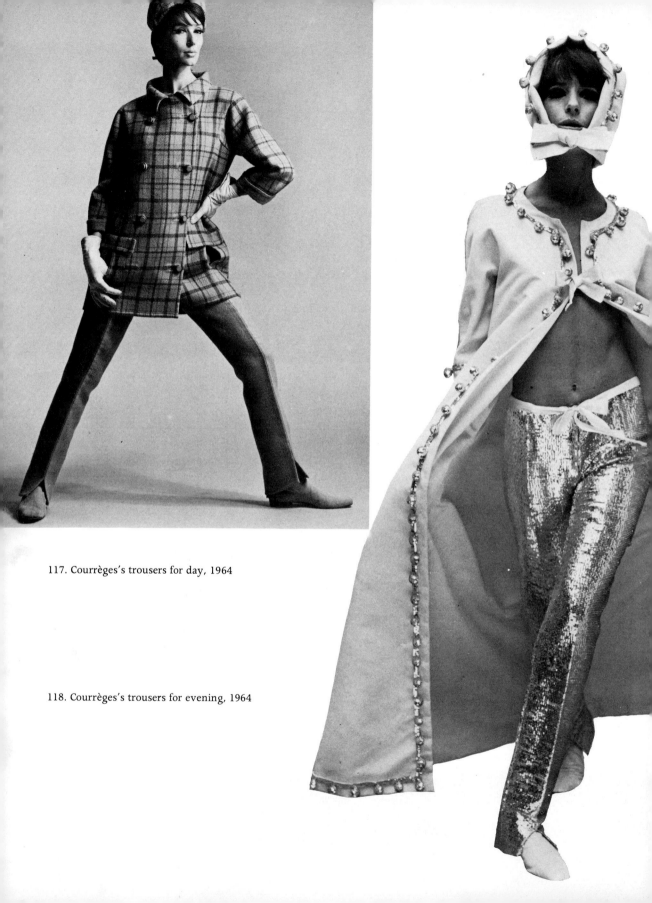

117. Courrèges's trousers for day, 1964

118. Courrèges's trousers for evening, 1964

120. Saint Laurent's smoking and city pants, 1967

119. Early "smoking", 1925

121. Culottes by Norman Norell, 1960

122. Culottes, 1924

123. Midi, mini by Jean Muir, 1967

124. Hair in the Sixties in Italy, 1966

125. Stockings by Valentino, 1968

126. Thigh boots and the Dr Zhivago look, by Grès, 1966

127. The see-through by Feraud, 1964

128. Sun specs take hold, 1965

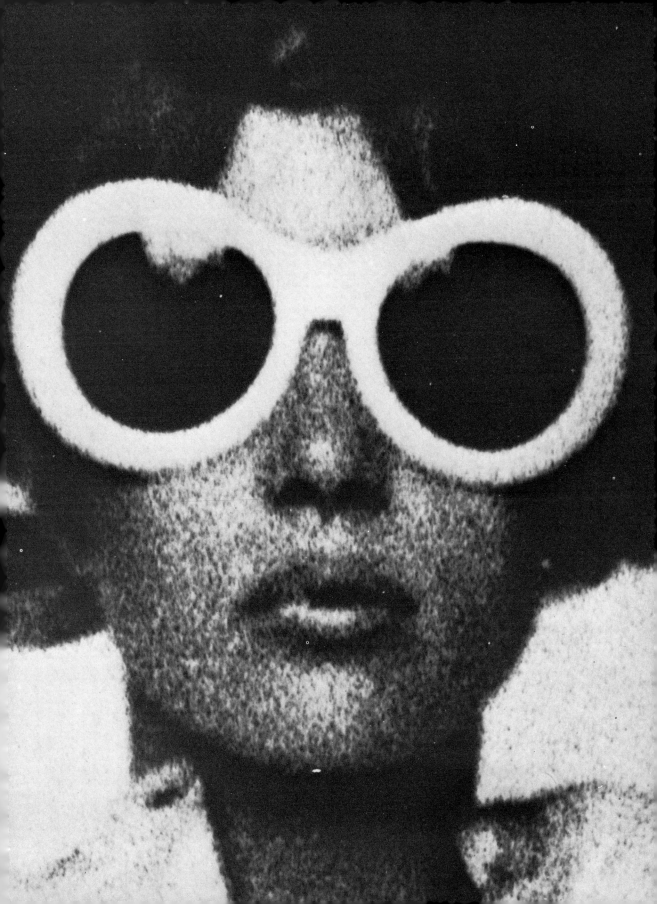

129. Madame Grès's famous draped jersey, 1961

130. Jean Shrimpton: the face of the '60s (Dress by John Bates)

131. King's Road, 1966

132. *below* Carnaby Street, 1967

133. *opposite* Bill Gibb, fantasist of fashion, 1969

134. Persian embroidery, gaucho hat, Zhivago boots,
by New York's Bill Blass, 1970

135. Straight from the steppes to New York,
by Oscar de la Renta, 1970

The Seventies

The Seventies began on the same wave of nostalgia, with the same desperate gleaning of ideas from ethnic dress, that had made the closing years of the Sixties so uninspired and uninspiring.

Collections seemed either like home movies of travels to distant lands—Turkestan, Morocco, Japan, Hungary, Persia, India, and above all Russia from whose bourne no fashion traveller has really returned since they followed Dr Zhivago there in 1966—or jejune pastiches of film costumes of the Twenties, Thirties, Forties. . . .

The most damaging change in fashion had been the midi—damaging because the sudden lengthening of skirts superannuated clothes already in the shops, leaving retailers with unsaleable stock, and because the uncertain manner with which the designers presented the new length persuaded women to take refuge in trousers.

Except for a brief flirtation with hot pants, originated by Mary Quant, skirts remained long. Swinging London of the Sixties became Docile London in the Seventies, following the Paris ready-to-wear led by Yves Saint Laurent and Karl Lagerfeld of Chloe into a uniform of droopy skirts, shapeless smocks, voluminous coats, muffling scarves and the inevitable boots. The sleeve on sleeve introduced by Gérard Pipart at Nina Ricci in the Sixties became an ubiquitous cliché.

136. Hot pants as Ungaro saw them,
drawn by Benais, 1971 . . .

137. Hot pants as worn, Paris, 1973

The French Couture, its already waning prestige further
weakened by Balenciaga's retirement, has only Givenchy and
Marc Bohan at Dior to uphold its great traditions. In London the
Couture is reduced to two Dressmakers to the Queen, Norman
Hartnell and Hardy Amies, but the many ready-to-wear de-
signers have established themselves.

In London the late Sixties had produced two violently contrasting boutique phenomena: Biba and Laura Ashley. By the
early Seventies Biba's vampish Thirties decadence and Laura
Ashley's Edwardian milkmaid innocence had made each a
lodestone for tourists as well as for the young at home.

A few new talents have appeared. In Paris Jap sped across the
fashion firmament like a tiny comet, with Sonia Rykiel and
Missoni of Italy, giving knitwear a new lease of life. London
has its own Japanese in Yuki, an Oriental Madame Grès, while
New York has Halston, milliner turned dress designer.

But no one has emerged of the stature of the giants of the past:
Poiret, Vionnet, Chanel, Schiaparelli, Dior, Balenciaga, designers
who changed the course of fashion. Nor has there been another
personality as potent as Mary Quant, who put her label on a
decade.

138. Trousers as Dior saw them 1972 . . .

139. Trousers as they are worn 1973

140. opposite Yves Saint Laurent back to the steppes again, 1974

142. Missoni knits stripes and zigzags, 1974

141. Karl Lagerfeld at Chloe tops the midi with the smock, 1974

143. Valentino pleats knits, 1974

144. Jap shapes one of his own prints, 1974

145. Biba's naughty Thirties Look, 1974

146. Laura Ashley's milkmaid Look, 1975

147. Thea Porter: a bow to the Middle East, 1974

148. Gina Fratini, artist of the pretty, 1970

149. Zandra Rhodes's contrasting patterns and plai[n]
bodice became the vernacular of the King's Road,
1970

150. Bill Gibb toes the line: voluminous coat, scarf and boots, 1975

151. Jean Muir, classicist, back to culottes, 1975

152. *overleaf* John Bates floats into 1975